Lipton Soup Mix Magic

Including One-Dish Meals and Slow Cooker Recipes

Lipton Lipton® Onion Dip

1 envelope LIPTON® RECIPE SECRETS® Onion Soup Mix
1 container (16 ounces) sour cream

1. In medium bowl, combine ingredients; chill, if desired.

2. Serve with your favorite dippers.   *Makes 2 cups dip*

Salsa Onion Dip: Stir in ½ cup of your favorite salsa.

Prep Time: 5 minutes

Lipton Lipton® Ranch Dip

1 envelope LIPTON® RECIPE SECRETS® Ranch Soup Mix
1 container (16 ounces) sour cream

1. In medium bowl, combine ingredients; chill, if desired.

2. Serve with your favorite dippers.   *Makes 2 cups dip*

Ranch Salsa Dip: Stir in ½ cup of your favorite salsa.

Ranch Artichoke Dip: Stir in 1 jar (14 ounces) marinated artichoke hearts, drained and chopped.

Prep Time: 5 minutes

Top to bottom: Lipton® Onion Dip & Lipton® Ranch Dip

Lipton. 7-Layer Ranch Dip

1 envelope LIPTON® RECIPE SECRETS® Ranch Soup Mix
1 container (16 ounces) sour cream
1 cup shredded lettuce
1 medium tomato, chopped (about 1 cup)
1 can (2.25 ounces) sliced pitted ripe olives, drained
¼ cup chopped red onion
1 can (4.5 ounces) chopped green chilies, drained
1 cup shredded Cheddar cheese (about 4 ounces)

1. In 2-quart shallow dish, combine soup mix and sour cream.

2. Evenly layer remaining ingredients, ending with cheese. Chill, if desired. Serve with tortilla chips.   *Makes 7 cups dip*

Prep Time: 15 minutes

Lipton. Vegetable Cream Cheese

1 envelope LIPTON® RECIPE SECRETS® Vegetable Soup Mix
2 packages (8 ounces each) cream cheese, softened
2 tablespoons milk

1. In medium bowl, combine ingredients; chill 2 hours.

2. Serve on bagels or with assorted fresh vegetables.

Makes 2½ cups spread

Prep Time: 10 minutes
Chill Time: 2 hours

7-Layer Ranch Dip

Lipton Party Stuffed Pinwheels

1 envelope LIPTON® RECIPE SECRETS® Savory Herb with Garlic Soup Mix*
1 package (8 ounces) cream cheese, softened
1 cup shredded mozzarella cheese (about 4 ounces)
2 tablespoons milk
1 tablespoon grated Parmesan cheese
2 packages (10 ounces each) refrigerated pizza crust

*Also terrific with LIPTON® RECIPE SECRETS® Onion Soup Mix.

1. Preheat oven to 425°F. In medium bowl, combine all ingredients except pizza crusts; set aside.

2. Unroll pizza crusts, then top evenly with filling. Roll, starting at longest side, jelly-roll style. Cut into 32 rounds.**

3. On baking sheet sprayed with nonstick cooking spray, arrange rounds cut side down.

4. Bake, uncovered, 13 minutes or until golden brown.

Makes 32 pinwheels

**If rolled pizza crust is too soft to cut, refrigerate or freeze until firm.

Lipton Vegetable Potato Salad

1 envelope LIPTON® RECIPE SECRETS® Vegetable Soup Mix
1 cup HELLMANN'S® or BEST FOODS® Mayonnaise
2 teaspoons white vinegar
2 pounds red or all-purpose potatoes, cooked and cut into chunks
¼ cup finely chopped red onion (optional)

1. In large bowl, combine soup mix, mayonnaise and vinegar.

2. Add potatoes and onion; toss well. Chill 2 hours.

Makes 6 servings

Prep Time: 20 minutes
Chill Time: 2 hours

Party Stuffed Pinwheels

Lipton Hearty Nachos

1 pound ground beef
1 envelope LIPTON® RECIPE SECRETS® Onion Soup Mix
1 can (19 ounces) black beans, rinsed and drained
1 cup prepared salsa
1 package (8½ ounces) plain tortilla chips
1 cup shredded Cheddar cheese (about 4 ounces)

1. In 12-inch nonstick skillet, brown ground beef over medium-high heat; drain.

2. Stir in soup mix, black beans and salsa. Bring to a boil over high heat. Reduce heat to low and simmer 5 minutes or until heated through.

3. Arrange tortilla chips on serving platter. Spread beef mixture over chips; sprinkle with Cheddar cheese. Top, if desired, with sliced green onions, sliced pitted ripe olives, chopped tomato and chopped cilantro. *Makes 8 servings*

Prep Time: 10 minutes
Cook Time: 12 minutes

Lipton Creamy Ranch Dressing

1 envelope LIPTON® RECIPE SECRETS® Ranch Soup Mix
**1 cup HELLMANN'S® or BEST FOODS® Mayonnaise or 1 cup
    sour cream**
½ cup milk

1. In medium bowl, combine all ingredients. Chill 30 minutes.

2. Serve as dressing for salads and sandwiches.

Makes 1½ cups

Serving Suggestions: Pour dressing over salad greens; use in your favorite pasta or potato salad; use as dressing for wraps and sandwiches.

Prep Time: 5 minutes
Chill Time: 30 minutes

Hearty Nachos

Lipton Hot Artichoke Dip

1 envelope LIPTON® RECIPE SECRETS® Onion Soup Mix*
1 can (14 ounces) artichoke hearts, drained and chopped
1 cup HELLMANN'S® or BEST FOODS® Mayonnaise
1 container (8 ounces) sour cream
1 cup shredded Swiss or mozzarella cheese (about
4 ounces)

*Also terrific with LIPTON® RECIPE SECRETS® Savory Herb with Garlic, Golden Onion, or Onion Mushroom Soup Mix.

1. Preheat oven to 350°F. In 1-quart casserole, combine all ingredients.

2. Bake uncovered 30 minutes or until heated through.

3. Serve with your favorite dippers.   *Makes 3 cups dip*

Cold Artichoke Dip: Omit Swiss cheese. Stir in, if desired, ¼ cup grated Parmesan cheese. Do not bake.

Prep Time: 5 minutes
Bake Time: 30 minutes

Recipe Tip

When serving hot dip for a party, try baking it in 2 smaller casseroles. When the first casserole is empty, replace it with the second one, fresh from the oven.

Hot Artichoke Dip

Lipton Savory Chicken Satay

1 envelope LIPTON® RECIPE SECRETS® Onion Soup Mix
¼ cup BERTOLLI® Olive Oil
2 tablespoons firmly packed brown sugar
2 tablespoons SKIPPY® Peanut Butter
1 pound boneless, skinless chicken breasts, pounded and
    cut into thin strips
12 to 16 large wooden skewers, soaked in water

1. In large plastic bag, combine soup mix, oil, brown sugar and peanut butter. Add chicken and toss to coat well. Close bag and marinate in refrigerator 30 minutes.

2. Remove chicken from marinade, discarding marinade. On skewers, thread chicken, weaving back and forth.

3. Grill or broil chicken until chicken is thoroughly cooked. Serve with your favorite dipping sauces.

Makes 12 to 16 appetizers

Prep Time: 15 minutes
Marinate Time: 30 minutes
Cook Time: 8 minutes

Lipton Salsa Onion Dip

1 envelope LIPTON® RECIPE SECRETS® Onion Soup Mix
1 container (16 ounces) sour cream
½ cup salsa

1. In medium bowl, combine ingredients; chill, if desired.

2. Serve with your favorite dippers.   *Makes 2½ cups dip*

Prep Time: 5 minutes

Savory Chicken Satay

Lipton Onion-Apple Glazed Pork Tenderloin

1 (1½- to 2-pound) boneless pork tenderloin
  Ground black pepper
2 tablespoons BERTOLLI® Olive Oil, divided
1 envelope LIPTON® RECIPE SECRETS® Onion Soup Mix
½ cup apple juice
2 tablespoons firmly packed brown sugar
¾ cup water
¼ cup dry red wine or water
1 tablespoon all-purpose flour

1. Preheat oven to 425°F. In small roasting pan or baking pan, arrange pork. Season with pepper and rub with 1 tablespoon olive oil. Roast uncovered 10 minutes.

2. Meanwhile, in small bowl, combine remaining 1 tablespoon olive oil, soup mix, apple juice and brown sugar. Pour over pork and continue roasting 10 minutes or until desired doneness. Remove pork to serving platter; cover with aluminum foil.

3. Place roasting pan over medium-high heat and bring pan juices to a boil, scraping up any browned bits from bottom of pan. Stir in water, wine and flour; boil, stirring constantly, 1 minute or until thickened.

4. To serve, thinly slice pork and serve with gravy.

Makes 4 to 6 servings

Prep Time: 5 minutes
Cook Time: 25 minutes

Onion-Apple Glazed Pork Tenderloin

Lipton Herbed Chicken & Vegetables

2 medium all-purpose potatoes, thinly sliced (about
    1 pound)
2 medium carrots, sliced
4 bone-in chicken pieces (about 2 pounds)
1 envelope LIPTON® RECIPE SECRETS® Savory Herb
    with Garlic Soup Mix
⅓ cup water
1 tablespoon BERTOLLI® Olive Oil

1. Preheat oven to 425°F. In broiler pan without the rack, place potatoes and carrots; arrange chicken on top. Pour soup mix blended with water and oil over chicken and vegetables.

2. Bake uncovered 40 minutes or until chicken is thoroughly cooked and vegetables are tender.   *Makes 4 servings*

Slow Cooker Method: In slow cooker, layer potatoes, carrots then chicken. Pour soup mix blended with water and oil over chicken and vegetables. Cook covered on HIGH 4 hours or LOW 6 to 8 hours.

Prep Time: 10 minutes
Cook Time: 40 minutes

Herbed Chicken & Vegetables

Lipton Souperior Meat Loaf

2 pounds ground beef
¾ cup plain dry bread crumbs*
1 envelope LIPTON® RECIPE SECRETS® Onion Soup Mix**
¾ cup water
⅓ cup ketchup
2 eggs

Substitution: Use 1½ cups fresh bread crumbs or 5 slices fresh bread, cubed.

Also terrific with LIPTON® RECIPE SECRETS® Beefy Onion, Onion Mushroom, Beefy Mushroom or Savory Herb with Garlic Soup Mix.

1. Preheat oven to 350°F. In large bowl, combine all ingredients.

2. In 13×9-inch baking or roasting pan, shape into loaf.

3. Bake uncovered 1 hour or until done. Let stand 10 minutes before serving.   *Makes 8 servings*

Slow Cooker Method: In slow cooker, arrange meat. Cook covered on HIGH for 4 hours or LOW 6 to 8 hours.

Helpful Hint: Placing meat loaf on a piece of cheesecloth and then on a rack helps to hold the meat together while lifting in and out of slow cooker.

Recipe Tip: It's a snap to make fresh bread crumbs. Simply process fresh or day old white, Italian or French bread in a food processor or blender until fine crumbs form.

Prep Time: 10 minutes
Cook Time: 1 hour

Souperior Meat Loaf and Ranch Mashed Potatoes (page 30)

Lipton Oven-Baked Stew

2 pounds boneless beef chuck or round steak, cut into 1-inch cubes
¼ cup all-purpose flour
1⅓ cups sliced carrots
1 can (14 to 16 ounces) whole peeled tomatoes, undrained and chopped
1 envelope LIPTON® RECIPE SECRETS® Onion Soup Mix*
½ cup dry red wine or water
1 cup fresh or canned sliced mushrooms
1 package (8 ounces) medium or broad egg noodles, cooked and drained

Also terrific with LIPTON® RECIPE SECRETS® Beefy Onion, Onion Mushroom or Beefy Mushroom Soup Mix.

1. Preheat oven to 425°F. In 2½-quart shallow casserole, toss beef with flour, then bake uncovered 20 minutes, stirring once.

2. *Reduce heat to 350°F.* Stir in carrots, tomatoes, soup mix and wine.

3. Bake covered 1½ hours or until beef is tender. Stir in mushrooms and bake covered an additional 10 minutes. Serve over hot noodles. *Makes 8 servings*

Slow Cooker Method: In slow cooker, toss beef with flour. Add carrots, tomatoes, soup mix and wine. Cook covered on LOW 8 to 10 hours. Add mushrooms; cook covered on LOW 30 minutes or until beef is tender. Serve over hot noodles.

Prep Time: 20 minutes
Cook Time: 2 hours

Oven-Baked Stew

Lipton Cheesy Garlic Chicken

4 boneless, skinless chicken breast halves (about 1¼ pounds)
1 medium tomato, coarsely chopped
1 envelope LIPTON® RECIPE SECRETS® Savory Herb with Garlic Soup Mix
⅓ cup water
1 tablespoon BERTOLLI® Olive Oil
1 cup shredded mozzarella cheese (about 4 ounces)
1 tablespoon grated Parmesan cheese

1. Preheat oven to 400°F. In 13×9-inch baking dish, arrange chicken; top with tomato.

2. Pour soup mix blended with water and oil over chicken.

3. Bake uncovered 20 minutes. Top with cheeses and bake 5 minutes or until cheese is melted and chicken is thoroughly cooked. Serve, if desired, with crusty Italian bread.

Makes 4 servings

Recipe Tip: Turn leftover Cheesy Garlic Chicken into a quick and delicious lunch or dinner. Simply heat and serve on hot store-bought garlic bread.

Prep Time: 5 minutes
Cook Time: 25 minutes

Cheesy Garlic Chicken

Lipton | Savory Skillet Broccoli

1 tablespoon BERTOLLI® Olive Oil
6 cups fresh broccoli florets *or* 1 pound green beans,
    trimmed
1 envelope LIPTON® RECIPE SECRETS® Golden Onion
    Soup Mix*
1½ cups water

Also terrific with LIPTON® RECIPE SECRETS® Onion Mushroom Soup Mix.

1. In 12-inch skillet, heat oil over medium-high heat and cook broccoli, stirring occasionally, 2 minutes.

2. Stir in soup mix blended with water. Bring to a boil over high heat.

3. Reduce heat to medium-low and simmer covered 6 minutes or until broccoli is tender.   *Makes 4 servings*

Prep Time: 5 minutes
Cook Time: 10 minutes

Lipton | Garlic Fries

1 bag (32 ounces) frozen French fried potatoes
1 envelope LIPTON® RECIPE SECRETS® Savory Herb with
    Garlic Soup Mix*

Also terrific with LIPTON® RECIPE SECRETS® Onion Soup Mix.

1. Preheat oven to 450°F. In large bowl, thoroughly toss frozen French fried potatoes with soup mix; spread on jelly-roll pan.

2. Bake until golden and crisp, about 25 minutes, stirring once.
          Makes 4 servings

Prep Time: 5 minutes
Cook Time: 25 minutes

Savory Skillet Broccoli

Lipton Easy Fried Rice

¼ cup BERTOLLI® Olive Oil
4 cups cooked rice
2 cloves garlic, finely chopped
1 envelope LIPTON® RECIPE SECRETS® Onion Mushroom
   Soup Mix
½ cup water
1 tablespoon soy sauce
1 cup frozen peas and carrots, partially thawed
2 eggs, lightly beaten

1. In 12-inch nonstick skillet, heat oil over medium-high heat and cook rice, stirring constantly, 2 minutes or until rice is heated through. Stir in garlic.

2. Stir in soup mix blended with water and soy sauce and cook 1 minute. Stir in peas and carrots and cook 2 minutes or until heated through.

3. Make a well in center of rice and quickly stir in eggs until cooked.   *Makes 4 servings*

Prep Time: 10 minutes
Cook Time: 10 minutes

Recipe Tip

For Simple Savory Rice, in 2-quart saucepan, bring 2½ cups water to a boil. Stir in 1 envelope Lipton Recipe Secrets Soup Mix (any variety) and 1 cup uncooked regular or converted rice. Simmer covered 20 minutes or until rice is tender.

Easy Fried Rice

Lipton | Lipton® Onion Burgers

1 envelope LIPTON® RECIPE SECRETS® Onion Soup Mix*
2 pounds ground beef
½ cup water

*Also terrific with LIPTON® RECIPE SECRETS® Beefy Onion, Onion Mushroom, Beefy Mushroom, Savory Herb with Garlic or Ranch Soup Mix.

1. In large bowl, combine all ingredients; shape into 8 patties.

2. Grill or broil until done.   *Makes about 8 servings*

Prep Time: 10 minutes
Cook Time: 12 minutes

Lipton | Ranch Mashed Potatoes

4 medium all-purpose potatoes, peeled, if desired, and cut into chunks (about 2 pounds)
1 envelope LIPTON® RECIPE SECRETS® Ranch Soup Mix
½ cup sour cream
½ cup milk
2 tablespoons margarine or butter, softened
2 slices bacon, crisp-cooked and crumbled *or* 2 tablespoons bacon bits (optional)

1. In 3-quart saucepan, cover potatoes with water. Bring to a boil.

2. Reduce heat to low and simmer 20 minutes or until potatoes are very tender; drain.

3. Return potatoes to saucepan; mash. Stir in remaining ingredients.   *Makes 6 servings*

Prep Time: 10 minutes
Cook Time: 25 minutes